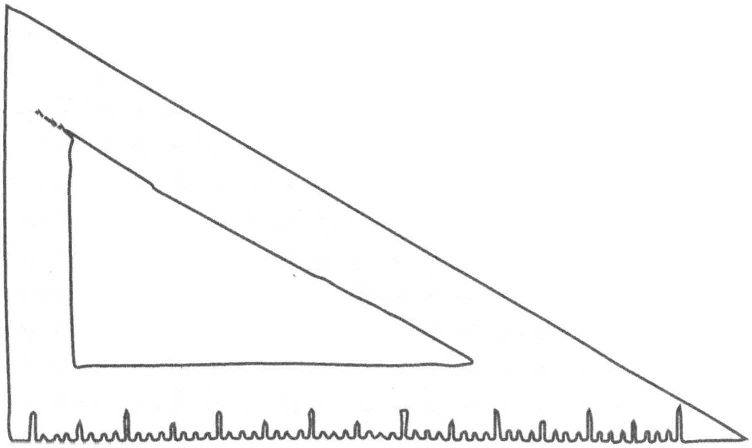

This Notebook Belongs To:

Subject:

Grade:

Made in the USA
Middletown, DE
19 July 2023

35431929R00064